History of Britain

The Home Front

1939 to 1945

Andrew Langley

Illustrated by John James

HISTORY OF BRITAIN – THE HOME FRONT
was produced for Heinemann Children's Reference
by Lionheart Books, London

Editor: Lionel Bender
Designer: Ben White
Editorial Assistant: Madeleine Samuel
Picture Researcher: Jennie Karrach
Media Conversion and Typesetting:
  Peter MacDonald

Educational Consultant: Jane Shuter
Editorial Advisors: Andrew Farrow, Paul Shuter

Production Controller: David Lawrence
Editorial Director: David Riley

First published in Great Britain in 1995
by Hamlyn Children's Books,
This edition published in Great Britain in 1996
by Heinemann Children's Reference, an imprint
of Heinemann Educational Publishers, a division of Reed
Educational and Professional Publishing Limited,
Halley Court, Jordan Hill, Oxford OX2 8EJ

MADRID ATHENS PARIS
FLORENCE PRAGUE WARSAW
PORTSMOUTH NH CHICAGO SAO PAULO
SINGAPORE TOKYO MELBOURNE AUCKLAND
IBADAN GABORONE JOHANNESBURG

ISBN 0 600 58601 4 Hb   ISBN 0 600 58602 2 Pb

British Library Cataloguing-in-Publication Data.
A catalogue record for this book is available
from the British Library.

Printed in Hong Kong

Acknowledgements
All artwork by John James
Map on page 23 by Hayward Art Group.

Photo credits
Topham Picture Library: pages 4 (left), 5, 6 (bottom), 10
(bottom centre, top), 18, 22 (top, bottom). Hulton Deutsch
Collection: pages 4-5, 7 (bottom), 8, 10-11, 11 (top), 12
(bottom), 13 (top), 14-15 (all photos), 16, 17 (top), 19 (top,
centre right), 20-21 (all photos). Robert Opie Collection: pages
4 (top, centre), 6 (top left, top right), 9 (right), 12-13 (centre),
13 (bottom), 16-17 (top: with Gunnersbury Park Museum,
London). Imperial War Museum, London: pages 7 (top: artist
A. Games), 9 (left, centre). Syndication International: page 17
(bottom). British Film Institute: page 19 (left) – Still from the
film "IN WHICH WE SERVE" by courtesy of The Rank
Organization plc.
Cover: Icon artwork by Jonathan Adams. Cover photos: Land
girl on tractor – Hulton Deutsch Collection. Poster and ration
books – Robert Opie Collection. Food banners – e.t. archive.
Evacuees – Hulton Deutsch Collection.

PLACES TO VISIT

Here are some museums and sites which contain exhibits
about the Home Front. Your local tourist office will be able to
tell you about places to visit in your area. Throughout 1995
there will be special events and exhibitions celebrating the
50th anniversary of the end of World War II.

Cabinet War Rooms, London. The underground rooms from
which the Government ran Britain during the War.

Caernarfon Air World, Gwynedd. Includes several World War
II aircraft, with a special Dambusters exhibit.

Coventry Cathedral. A fine new cathedral, completed in
1964 next to the bombed shell of the old one.

Dover Castle and Hellfire Corner, Kent. Beneath the old
castle is a maze of tunnels where the Dunkirk evacuation
was planned.

Duxford Airfield, Cambridge. The Imperial War Museum's
collection of historic aircraft also includes a reconstruction
of a wartime air raid.

HMS Belfast, London. The largest surviving World War II
warship used to support the D-Day landings.

Imperial War Museum, London. Among many special
exhibits are features on the Blitz and the Home Front.

Station 146, Norfolk. Preserved wartime control tower once
used by a US Air Force squadron.

Tangmere Military Aviation Museum, Sussex. A famous
Battle of Britain airfield.

Western Approaches, Liverpool. Re-creation of the wartime
bunker where the campaign against German U-boats was
organized.

White Cliffs Experience, Dover. This multi-media show
includes a simulation of an air raid.

Winston Churchill's Britain at War Museum, London. Many
exhibits about the Home Front, with many sound effects.

INTRODUCTION

During the late 1930s, Germany was ruled by Adolf Hitler and the Nazis. Hitler wanted to build an empire in Europe. In 1938, his troops took over Austria. In March 1939, they marched into Czechoslovakia. Six months later they invaded Poland.

This alarmed the governments of Britain and France. They told Hitler that he must withdraw his troops from Poland. Hitler refused, so on 3 September the British and French declared war on Germany. This, the Second World War, lasted until 1945 and was fought over much of Europe and Asia. There were no land battles in Britain. Even so, everyone there had to play a part in the war effort, sharing dangers and hardships. This was known as the Home Front.

CONTENTS

STANDING ALONE 4

A gas mask and its box

RATIONING 6

A family's weekly ration of meat

ALIENS AND SPIES 8

A BBC radio microphone

THE HOME FRONT 10

A barrage balloon

DIG FOR VICTORY 12

A tin of cocoa, a bar of chocolate

WOMEN AT WAR 14

A servicewoman in uniform

CHILDREN AT WAR 16

A baby's gas mask

KEEPING CHEERFUL 18

A newspaper billboard

THE G.I.S AND D-DAY 20

A US airman's shoulder badge

BACK TO NORMAL 22

A 'demob' suit of 1945

GLOSSARY – DEFINITIONS OF IMPORTANT WORDS 23

TIMECHART 23

INDEX 24

STANDING ALONE

"I have nothing to offer but blood, toil, tears and sweat. You ask, What is our aim? I can answer in one word: Victory." This is part of a speech made by Winston Churchill when he became Prime Minister in May 1940. But then, victory seemed a long way off.

The German forces had already conquered Norway and Denmark. Now, they were sweeping through Belgium and the Netherlands. By 20 May, they reached the English Channel. More than 500,000 British and French troops were trapped on the French coast at Dunkirk. Hundreds of boats, big and small, repeatedly sailed from Britain to rescue them, and brought nearly 340,000 safely back to England. The German advance went on. On 17 June France surrendered. Most of north-west Europe was now in Hitler's hands. The German leader began to plan the invasion of Britain, only 34 kilometres away.

△ ▽ **Posters urging people to join** the army or the ARP (Air Raid Precautions) units at home. In September 1939, people were already busy preparing for war:
● gas masks were issued, to wear in case of gas attacks
● air raid shelters were built
● sandbags were piled round buildings to protect against bombs
● white lines were painted on roads to prevent accidents in the blackout.

△ **An AA (Anti-Aircraft) battery** is set up at Ladywell, London, in 1939. These guns hit very few German bombers, but the noise of their firing encouraged people sheltering from the Blitz.

▷ **Children being evacuated** (sent away). When war broke out, over 1.5 million mothers and children left the big towns. They were housed in the countryside, to be safe from the bombs.

4

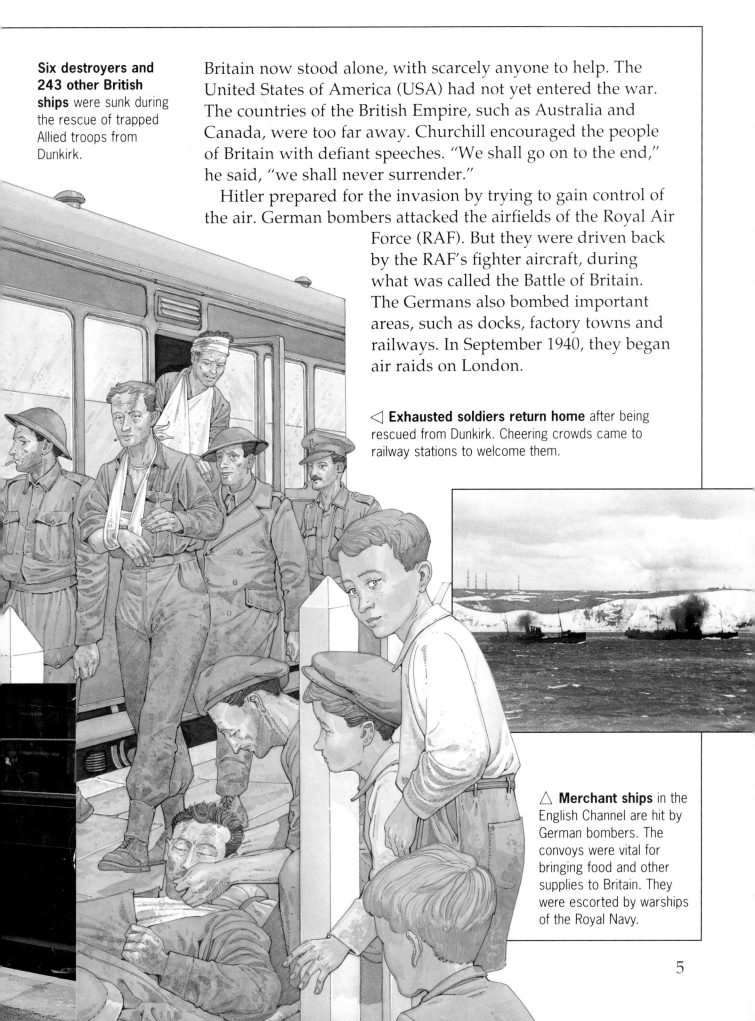

Six destroyers and 243 other British ships were sunk during the rescue of trapped Allied troops from Dunkirk.

Britain now stood alone, with scarcely anyone to help. The United States of America (USA) had not yet entered the war. The countries of the British Empire, such as Australia and Canada, were too far away. Churchill encouraged the people of Britain with defiant speeches. "We shall go on to the end," he said, "we shall never surrender."

Hitler prepared for the invasion by trying to gain control of the air. German bombers attacked the airfields of the Royal Air Force (RAF). But they were driven back by the RAF's fighter aircraft, during what was called the Battle of Britain. The Germans also bombed important areas, such as docks, factory towns and railways. In September 1940, they began air raids on London.

◁ **Exhausted soldiers return home** after being rescued from Dunkirk. Cheering crowds came to railway stations to welcome them.

△ **Merchant ships** in the English Channel are hit by German bombers. The convoys were vital for bringing food and other supplies to Britain. They were escorted by warships of the Royal Navy.

RATIONING

The sea was a natural barrier for the British against the Germans. But it also caused problems. Britain's farmers could not grow enough food to feed the population. Large amounts had to be brought in from abroad by ship.

△ **An adult's weekly ration of food**, and ration books and coupons in 1942-1943. Rations were provided by the Ministry of Food and Board of Trade.

▽ **A bus which is powered by gas** from the trailer behind. It was used to save petrol. Many people began to travel by horse and cart instead of by car.

The slow and lightly armed merchant, or goods, ships were easy targets for German U-boats (submarines) and bomber aircraft. Between March and May 1941, over 320 merchant ships bound for Britain were sunk. Foods such as flour, meat and sugar were in short supply.

The government had been prepared for this. They decided to ration (limit) the amount of certain goods people could buy to make supplies last longer. Soon after war broke out, ration books were issued to everyone. These contained coupons, which a shopkeeper cut out when an item was purchased to ensure no one could buy more than their share. Butter, meat and fresh eggs were among the first foods to be rationed. In their place, people were encouraged to use margarine, corned beef and dried egg powder.

▷ **Queues at a grocery shop.** This was the weekly ration for one person in 1941:
● 1 ounce (28 grams) of cheese and 4 ounces (112 grams) of butter
● 2 ounces (56 grams) of tea
● 12 ounces (336 grams) of sugar
● 3 pints of milk
● 1 packet of dried egg
● 1 shilling 2 pence (value about £2 today) worth of meat.
Rations changed as supplies of goods varied.

Rationing for clothes began in June 1941. Every person was allowed 66 clothing coupons for a whole year. A woman's woollen dress needed 11 coupons, and shoes needed 5. For a three-piece suit, a man had to hand over 26 coupons. But, even with rationing, cloth and other materials were scarce.

Several other important items were rationed, including soap and petrol for cars. Supplies of coal often ran short, as there were not enough miners to work the pits. People were asked to use less gas and electricity in their homes. Even items such as candles, ladies' stockings and kettles became hard to find.

◁ **The first day of rationing.** A woman hands over her ration book to buy food. The assistant cuts out the correct number of coupons. But shops were not the only place where scarce goods could be bought. 'Black market' dealers obtained food and clothes and then sold them secretly. Many black marketeers became very rich, though if caught they would be heavily fined or put in prison. So, too, would people who forged food, petrol or clothing coupons.

ALIENS AND SPIES

With the threat of invasion so near, people began to watch carefully for traitors, spies or enemy agents. Those most seriously suspected were the German and Austrian refugees. More than 60,000 of them had come to live in Britain. Most of them were Jews, who had fled from persecution in Germany.

▷ **Alien prisoners** are guarded by soldiers as they board a coach taking them to an internment camp in a remote part of western Britain. The government feared that, if there was an invasion, some aliens would help the enemy.

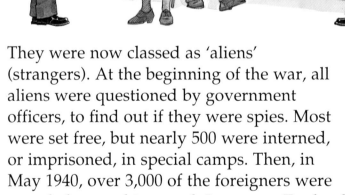

△ **William Joyce**, a supporter of the Nazi Party. He joined the Germans and made radio broadcasts from the Continent. Joyce tried to convince the British that they were losing the war. Most listeners made fun of his voice, and called him 'Lord Haw-Haw'.

They were now classed as 'aliens' (strangers). At the beginning of the war, all aliens were questioned by government officers, to find out if they were spies. Most were set free, but nearly 500 were interned, or imprisoned, in special camps. Then, in May 1940, over 3,000 of the foreigners were rounded up and interned. In eastern England, where links with Europe were hard to control, all other aliens were ordered to report to the police every day and to stay at home after dark.

Not only foreigners were under suspicion. The British politician Oswald Mosley was leader of the Union of Fascists. This organization supported many of Hitler's ideas, and wanted Britain to stay at peace with Germany. Mosley and 33 of his followers were arrested in June 1940 and kept in prison for the rest of the war.

Paſſierſchein

Der deutſche Soldat, der dieſen Paſſierſchein vorzeigt, bringt ihn als Zeichen ſeines ehrlichen Willens, ſich zu ergeben. Er iſt zu entwaffnen. Er muß gut behandelt werden. Er hat Anſpruch auf Verpflegung und, wenn nötig, ärztliche Behandlung. Er wird ſo bald wie möglich aus der Gefahrenzone entfernt.

Dwight D. Eisenhower

OBERBEFEHLSHABER
der alliierten Expeditions-Armeen

Engliſche Überſetzung nachſtehend. Sie dient als Anweiſung an die alliierten Vorpoſten.

SAFE CONDUCT

The German soldier who carries this safe conduct is using it as a sign of his genuine wish to give himself up. He is to be disarmed, to be well looked after, to receive food and medical attention as required, and to be removed from the danger zone as soon as possible.

Dwight D. Eisenhower

SUPREME COMMANDER,
Allied Expeditionary Force

Keep mum –
she's not
so dumb!

CARELESS TALK COSTS LIVES

There were many invasion scares during the summer of 1940. One person reported that German paratroopers had landed in Scotland – disguised as nuns! Another believed that spies had ray guns which stopped moving cars. The police threatened to arrest anyone who spread such rumours, which might cause a national panic.

The government started a campaign of 'propaganda' (advertising), to keep people believing in and working hard at the struggle against Germany. It also passed new emergency laws giving it more power to control everyday lives. Banks and arms (weapons) factories were run by the government. Strikes were forbidden. Workers in vital industries, such as mining, were discouraged from joining the armed forces.

△ **A poster warning soldiers not to discuss important information** even with their wives or girlfriends. ('Mum' means to keep silent). Letters from soldiers abroad were carefully read by a government 'censor'. The censor blanked out any information about where the writer was serving. Details such as this might be useful to the enemy.

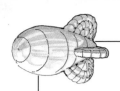

THE HOME GUARD

Frantically, Britain got ready to fight a German invasion. In May 1940, a new part-time army was formed – the Local Defence Volunteers (LDV). It called for recruits between the ages of 17 and 65. The LDV's name was soon changed to the Home Guard.

▷ **A pill box in Cumbria**, with a gun slot. The boxes were built so strongly that many of them still stand.

By July, there were over 1.5 million volunteers in this new force. Nearly all of them worked at other jobs by day. In their spare time they trained for combat, or guarded important sites such as railways, bridges and factories. The main job of the Home Guard was to resist landings by German parachute troops.

Daily life changed in many ways. Big houses and parks were taken over as military camps. Church bells could only be rung to warn of an invasion. A series of barriers was set up across the country to hold up enemy progress.

Concrete pill boxes, or shelters, were built to house guns and armed LDVs. Huge blocks and stones were placed on roads and fords ready to stop advancing tanks. Trenches in which soldiers could hide were dug on hill tops. Barbed wire was spread along the beaches of the south coast. Civilians were forbidden to go on sea fronts for their own safety.

▽ **An anti-aircraft machine gun unit near London** alongside the Thames. Huge barrage balloons were also floated over important targets to prevent German bombers from flying low.

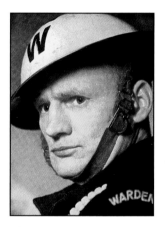

△ **An ARP warden** with protective helmet.

▷ **Women train with their rifles.** Though women did not join the Home Guard, some formed fighting units.

▷ **Disused cars and lorries** are spread across large flat fields in southern England to prevent enemy gliders from landing with troops. Broken-down vehicles and other large pieces of scrap metal were also collected and put ready to block main roads. Wire was stretched between posts across the widest roads so that they could not be used as runways for German aircraft.

Meanwhile, members of the part-time Observer Corps watched the skies and telephoned news of enemy aircraft to Army or RAF headquarters. The approach of aircraft could be spotted even earlier by the newly invented radar. Radio signals, sent out from tall metal masts, bounced off the aircraft and were picked up by a scanner.

▷ **Members of the Home Guard** take down road signs. Street name plates and sign posts – even for footpaths – were removed and stored during the war. This was done to confuse an invading army. Behind them is the ARP station and the first aid post (indicated by a red cross), which looked after casualties from bombing. It is protected from bomb blast by sandbags.

ARP ENQUIRIES

ARP
FIRST ✚ AID
DEPOT

REDHILL 3¼
REIGATE 4

DGE 5

EET ¼
3½

DIG FOR VICTORY

Because of rationing and German U-boats attacking merchant ships, people found their choice of food getting smaller. The only way to increase the supply was to produce more in Britain. This meant using extra areas of land to grow vegetables and fruit.

The biggest areas of new crops were on the farms. Grassland which had been grazed by cattle was ploughed up and sown with wheat, oats or potatoes. Altogether, an area of land bigger than Wales was dug up.

Market gardens also changed as vegetables were grown instead of flowers. Rose beds were replaced by rows of onions and carrots, and orchid houses by greenhouses full of tomatoes. Farmers and market gardeners were visited regularly by government inspectors to make sure that they were growing the most useful crops.

Householders were encouraged to grow as many of their own fruit and vegetables as possible. Not only were these a cheap source of nourishment, but it meant that other goods could be carried on cargo ships. Professional gardeners toured schools and gardening societies giving advice to beginners.

Parks, playing fields, village greens and roadside verges became 'allotments', which were small pieces of land rented to local people. By 1943, there were 3.5 million allotments in Britain, producing over a million tonnes of vegetables. Many people kept pigs and rabbits on their land to give extra meat, and chickens to provide eggs and meat.

▽ **Even the grounds of the Tower of London** (below) and small scraps of wasteland were used as vegetable gardens.

△ **Booklets from the Ministry of Food.** One gives people recipes. The other urges them to grow their own food.

▷ **Some bombed-out ruins made perfect places to keep pigs.** Pigs were easy to raise. They could be largely fed on old vegetables and other scraps boiled up as 'pigswill'.

◁ **A suburban garden in the summer of 1940.** The family stops gardening to watch RAF and German aircraft fighting above. Their small back garden is laid out with rows of beans, cabbages and other vegetables. Hens scratch outside their run. Rabbits are kept in a hutch next to the back door. Herbs are grown on top of the air raid shelter. In the background, a workman repairs blast damage to the roof.

▽ **Government leaflets on cooking.**

A KITCHEN GOES TO WAR

FAMOUS PEOPLE Contribute 150 Recipes to A RATION-TIME COOKERY BOOK

DRIED EGGS

MINISTRY OF FOOD WAR COOKERY LEAFLET 11

13

WOMEN AT WAR

The war brought a startling change to the lives of many women. Huge numbers of men were ordered by the government to serve in the armed forces. But their peacetime jobs still had to be done. So women went out to work – most for the first time.

One of the most vital industries was farming. The Women's Land Army was formed in 1939, calling for volunteers to take the place of thousands of male farmworkers. More than 100,000 women became 'Land Girls'. They did every kind of farm job, from sowing seeds, tending herds and harvesting crops to digging ditches and mending tractors.

Five million women also went to work in factories and shipyards. Many trained as machine operators or fitters. They learned to make parts for weapons, to assemble shells, tanks, aircraft and ships, and to weld metal.

△ **A nurse and a female rescue worker** clamber through rubble to help the wounded after a V-2 rocket landed in Farringdon Market, London, in March 1945.

As the war went on, many more women were needed to join the work-force. In 1943, the government decided to conscript (call up) all available women between the ages of 18 and 50. Only mothers with young children were excused war work. By this time, women were driving buses, loading trains, sweeping streets and delivering post and milk. Others joined the emergency services as ARP wardens, first aid nurses or cooks in mobile canteens.

△ **Land Girls hard at work on a farm.** They were paid the equivalent of about £20 a week, and were expected to work long hours.

▽ **A crew of WAAFs at a barrage balloon site** in London. In the foreground, mechanics repair a truck. The balloons had to be blown up with gas, raised into the sky and then tethered to the ground. By 1942, nearly half of all balloon operators were women.

△ **A woman at work** in the machine shop of an engineering factory. There was a special training school in Slough for female machinists.

▷ **A woman pilot** gets ready to fly a fighter plane from the factory to an RAF airfield. Most new aircraft were delivered by these 'ferry pilots'.

Women were not allowed to fight in battle, but they could join the armed forces. Those in the Auxiliary Territorial Service (ATS) helped to direct anti-aircraft gunfire. Members of the Women's Auxiliary Air Force, the WAAFs, worked as mechanics on aircraft and operated barrage balloons. Women in the Women's Royal Naval Service – the Wrens – served on board ship and on shore as radio operators and ambulance drivers.

CHILDREN AT WAR

"They labelled me, addressed me and packed me off to the country." This is one man's memory of being evacuated at the start of the war. He was only 9 years old at the time. Like thousands of other children, he spent most of the war living far away from his parents.

△ **Children come out of brick air raid shelters** during a practice drill at a school in Wigan, near Manchester.

▷ **Children help their parents to salvage belongings** from their house, damaged by a bomb the night before. Despite the danger, many children wanted to share hardships with their families. Those who were 'bombed out' usually went to stay with relatives, or moved in with neighbours.

Wartime was very frightening and confusing for young children. Many of those in towns were evacuated to areas away from the dangers of German bombers. They were taken away by train, bus or even boat. They stayed in private houses in villages or country towns.

Many children never left the cities. They were soon joined by young evacuees who had grown homesick and went back to their parents. But life in the heavily bombed cities, such as London, Manchester, Liverpool and Plymouth, could be much more terrifying. Families spent the nights in public air raid shelters, or in tiny 'Anderson' shelters in their gardens.

Sweets were rationed, and there were fewer toys in the shops. But town children soon got used to playing among ruined buildings and streets blocked with rubble. They competed with each other in making collections of 'trophies' – pieces from bombs or crashed aircraft.

Other collections helped in the war effort. Some children gathered scrap metal, such as old pots and pans. This was taken to dumps. It was melted down and could be used in the manufacture of aircraft and weapons.

△ **Some of the comics, games, models and playing cards** produced for children during the war.

◁ **A teacher repairs** a boy's trousers at an open-air school for evacuated children.

▽ **Children play at being ARP wardens** on a bombsite.

KEEPING CHEERFUL

At the outbreak of war, the government ordered that cinemas, theatres and dance halls were to close after 6 o'clock each evening. This was when the blackout began. But they quickly realized that people needed entertainment to take their minds off the hardships of the war, so early in 1940, the ban was lifted.

Many theatres stayed shut all the same, especially in London. There was just one pantomime to be seen there in 1940. Only the shows at the Windmill Theatre ran all through the war. Its management boasted afterwards, "We never closed".

▷ **The team of the BBC radio comedy programme ITMA** ("*It's That Man Again*") during a live broadcast. They were led by Tommy Handley (here seated). The show first went on air in September 1939. Soon, more than 10 million listeners were tuning in every week. ITMA made fun of things which annoyed ordinary people, like rationing and nosey government officials.

Going to the cinema was a regular treat for many people. A large number went twice a week. Cinemas showed patriotic films set in wartime, as well as news programmes, and documentaries (real-life films) about the armed services. But the most popular films of all came from the USA. Love stories, comedies and gangster adventures helped viewers to forget the bombs for an evening.

However, the blackout and petrol rationing made it difficult to travel. Many people were forced to spend most evenings at home. There, they listened to the news, music and comedy programmes on the radio. Sales of 'wireless', or radio sets, soared. There was also a huge increase in the buying of books, newspapers and magazines, in spite of the paper shortage.

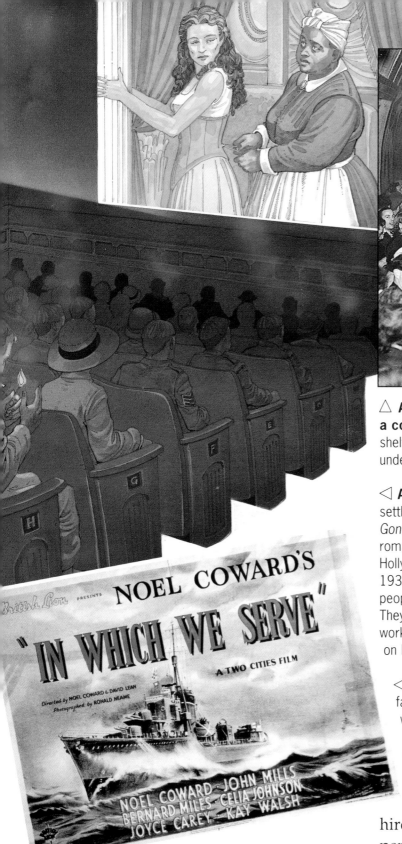

△ **An orchestra gives a concert** for people sheltering in an underground station.

◁ **A cinema audience** settles down to enjoy *Gone With the Wind*, a romantic drama made in Hollywood, USA, in 1938-39. Many of the people are in uniform. They are civil defence workers or servicemen on leave.

◁ **A poster** for a famous British patriotic wartime movie film.

△ **Vera Lynn**, the English popular music singer, was known as the Forces' Sweetheart.

Variety shows were also taken to people at work. The Entertainments National Service Association (ENSA) hired stars to travel the country performing in factory canteens and army barracks. The shows, called Workers' Playtime, were broadcast on the radio. The most popular stars were comedians, for example Max Miller and George Formby, and singers such as Vera Lynn.

THE G.I.S AND D-DAY

In 1940, when Italy, then Japan, allied with Germany, the war spread to Asia, the Mediterranean and North Africa. In December 1941, the Japanese attacked Pearl Harbor navy base in Hawaii, bringing the USA into the war on Britain's side. Within a few weeks, American troops began to arrive in Britain.

American soldiers were known as GIs. This was short for Government Issue, a term for their ordinary military clothing. But to most people in Britain, they seemed glamorous not ordinary. GIs were paid nearly three times as much as British soldiers. Their military stores were full of goods that were scarce in Britain, such as chocolate bars, nylon stockings, scented soap and cigarettes.

Special clubs opened near the American bases and in London. Here, the soldiers could drink Coca Cola, play pool and dance to the music of American big bands. The GIs quickly became very popular, especially with girls. During and soon after the war, 60,000 British girls married American servicemen.

△ **American soldiers hand out chewing gum** to village children before leaving for home in 1945.

▽ **A GI is invited to family tea by his girl friend.** He has brought presents for everyone – nylons, chocolate and sugar.

△ **The crew of a US Sherman tank** take part in a training exercise before D-Day in 1944.

◁ **An American GI and his girlfriend** at *Rainbow Corner*, one of the US clubs in London.

Altogether, over 1 million US troops came to Britain. They were joined by Canadian forces. Many were passing through, on their way to the fighting in Italy or North Africa. But others were preparing for Operation Overlord, or D-Day – the Allied invasion of France, to drive out the occupying German armies.

During early 1944, British, American and Canadian troops trained for the coming operation in secret locations all over the country. The roads and depots of southern England were cluttered with tanks, lorries and field guns.

At last, on 6 June, the D-Day invasion began. The US troops set off on landing craft from ports along the south-west coast, and the British and Canadians from the Hampshire and Sussex coasts. After a month of desperate fighting, they broke through the German lines.

△ **Everyday life goes on as lines of US jeeps, trucks and troop carriers** roar through the streets of an English town on their way to board ship for the D-Day landings. In the busiest places, GIs in white helmets and gloves directed the traffic.

GETTING BACK TO NORMAL

Throughout the summer of 1944, Allied troops pushed deeper into France. But soon after D-Day, the first German V-1s (flying bombs) fell on London. They were followed by V-2 rockets. These terrifying new weapons killed over 9,000 people.

▽ **Two weeks after VE-Day**, German prisoners are employed on a building site in South London to test the reaction of Londoners to their presence.

All the same, with German forces on the defensive, life in Britain was slowly getting easier. In September, the blackout rules were relaxed. Normal curtains were allowed at windows, and there were more street lights. Some road signs were replaced.

The Allies marched into Germany in February 1945. By March, they had captured most German airfields and rocket sites. The bombing 'blitz' on Britain was over at last and more food came from overseas. The war itself ended in May, when the Germans surrendered; 8 May was declared Victory in Europe (VE) Day. Celebrations were held throughout Britain.

◁ **The first men to be 'demobilized'** (released) from the RAF collect their official leaving papers on 18 June 1945. 'Demobbed' men were given civilian clothing. The first to be released were those who had served longest in the forces, or who had important jobs at home. To begin with, 30,000 men and women were demobbed each week. By December a million had left the services.

GLOSSARY

allied working and fighting together; referring to Britain and the Empire, France and the USA fighting against Germany, Italy and Japan.

Anderson shelter small air raid shelter made of corrugated iron sheets and covered with soil.

blitz a heavy bombing raid, from the German word *blitzkrieg* meaning lightning war; the first attacks were fast and took the Allies by surprise.

censor in wartime, someone who checks letters to make sure they contain no secret or important information.

coupon a small slip of paper which carries a certain ration value.

destroyer a medium-sized, fast warship.

empire a collection of territories ruled by a single country. The British Empire included Canada, Australia, India and much of eastern Africa, the West Indies and the Pacific Islands.

fascist somebody who believes that a country should be governed by a dictator (a ruler who has complete power).

identity card a card which bears a person's name and personal details similar to a passport.

radar a device for locating objects and following moving craft using radio signals.

recruit someone who has just joined one of the armed services.

refugee a person who leaves his or her own country to escape danger or bad treatment.

USA/US short for the United States of America/United States.

Britain in the Blitz. This map shows the main places which were hit by German bombs between May 1940 and March 1945.

Major cities bombed

SCOTLAND
Glasgow
Edinburgh
Newcastle
Sunderland
Belfast
Middlesborough
IRELAND
Liverpool
Manchester
Hull
Sheffield
Birmingham
Nottingham
WALES
Coventry
Norwich
Swansea
ENGLAND
Ipswich
Bristol
Cardiff
Bath
London
Southampton
Canterbury
Dunkirk
Exeter
Portsmouth
Calais
Plymouth

FRANCE

TIMECHART

1939
September 1: First people are evacuated from towns.
September 3: Britain declares war on Germany.

1940
January 8: Rationing of food begins.
May 9: Winston Churchill becomes Prime Minister.
May 15: The Local Defence Volunteers (Home Guard) is formed.
August 8: Battle of Britain begins.
September 7: First German bombing raid on London.

1941
December 8: The USA joins the Allies against Germany, Italy and Japan.

1942
March: 273 Allied merchant ships sunk by Germans.
August 17: The US Air Force Flying Fortresses (giant bombers) make their first raid on Europe.

1943
May 8: War work made compulsory for all British women aged 18 to 50.

1944
June 6: D-Day: Allied troops land in France.

1945
March: Last German air raids on Britain.
May 4: Germans surrender.
May 8: VE Day.
June 18: Demobilization of forces begins.

23

INDEX

ack-ack (AA) guns *see* anti-aircraft guns
aircraft
  enemy 11
  factories 15
airfields and runways 5, 11
Air Raid Precautions (ARP) 4, 11
  ARP wardens 10, 14, 17
air raid shelters 4, 13, 16, 17, 23
air raids 5, 23
aliens 8, 9
Allies, Allied Forces 21, 22, 23
allotments 12
anti-aircraft guns 4, 10
Australia 5
Austria 3
Auxiliary Territorial Service (ATS) 15

barrage balloons 10, 15
Battle of Britain 5, 23
Belgium 4
Black Market 7
blackout 4, 18, 22
bombers 23
  German 5, 6
  United States' 23
Britain 3, 4, 5
British Empire 5

Canada, Canadians 5, 21
censorship 9, 23
children 16, 17
Churchill, Winston 4, 5, 23
clothes 7
coupons, ration 6, 7, 23
Czechoslovakia 3

D-Day invasion 21, 23
demobilization 22, 23
Denmark 4
Dunkirk 4, 5

entertainment 18, 19
evacuation and evacuees 4, 16, 17, 23

factories 14, 15
farming 12, 13, 14
Fascists 8, 23
fighter aircraft 5, 15
food supplies 5, 6, 7, 12, 13, 22
forged documents 8
France and the French 3, 4

gardening (for food) 12, 13
gas mask 4
games (toys, comics) 17
Germany and the Germans 3, 4, 6, 8, 9, 20, 22
GIs 20

Hitler, Adolf 3, 5, 8
Home Guard 10, 11, 23

identity card 6, 23
internment (camps) 8
invasion (by German forces) 3, 4, 5, 8, 11
Italy 20

Japan 20
Jews 8
Joyce, William 8

laws 9
Liverpool 17

Local Defence Volunteers (LDV) *see* Home Guard
London 5, 17
Lord Haw-Haw *see* Joyce, William
Lynn, Vera 19

Manchester 17
market gardens 12
Mosley, Oswald 8

Nazis, the 3, 8
Netherlands, the 4
Norway 4

Observer Corps 11
Operation Overlord 21

parachute troops 10
Pearl Harbor 20
pill box 10
Plymouth 17
Poland and the Poles 3
propaganda 9

radar 11, 23
radio broadcasts 8, 18, 19
rationing 6, 7, 18, 23
refugees 8
road
  blocks 11
  signs 11, 22
rockets
  V1 22
  V2 14, 22
Royal Air Force (RAF) 5, 9, 22
Royal Navy 5

'safe conduct' leaflets 9
ships 5, 6
  merchant 5, 23

shipyards 14
shops, shopkeepers 7
soldiers 5, 20, 21 *see also* troops
spies 6, 8, 9

troops
  Allied 22
  American 20, 21
  British 4, 5
  Canadian 21
  French 4, 5
  German 3, 4, 10
'trophies'

U-boats 6, 7
USA (United States of America) 5, 20, 21, 23

VE (Victory in Europe) Day 22, 23

war work 14, 23
women 10, 14, 15, 23
Women's Auxiliary Air Force (WAAF) 15
Women's Land Army 14
Women's Royal Naval Service (Wrens) 15